HUSH, LITTLE ROCKET

New York Times–bestselling author Mo O'Hara

Illustrated by Alexandra Cook

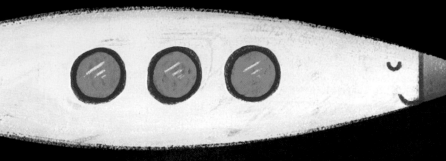

Feiwel and Friends
New York

Hush, Little Rocket, don't make a bleep.
We're heading home now; it's time to sleep.

You've played and raced the day away,
Swishing past stars in the Milky Way.

The sun's long flares shoot up so high
As you yawn and stretch with a sleepy sigh.

Each planet friend whispers, "Good night."

We'll pass them all on our bedtime flight.

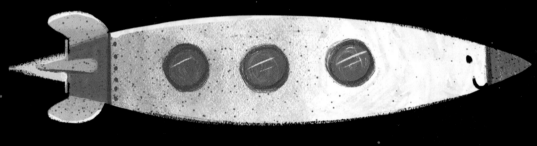

We swish through Mercury's dusty tail.

It turns slowly round like a little snail.

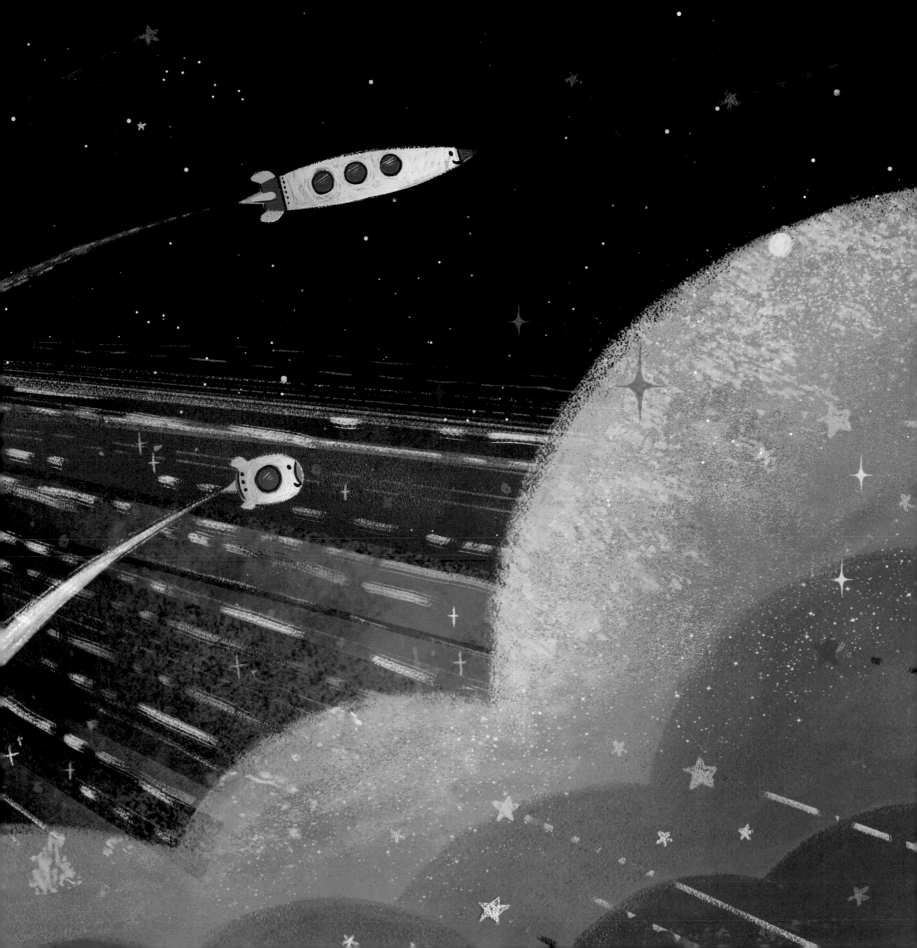

Venus shines like the brightest crown,

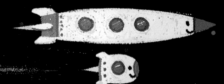

Spinning backward 'cause it's upside down.

Like a big blue marble, Earth rolls round.
We wish we could stop, but we're homeward bound.

The planet Mars is rusty red,
But the sunset's blue when it's time for bed.

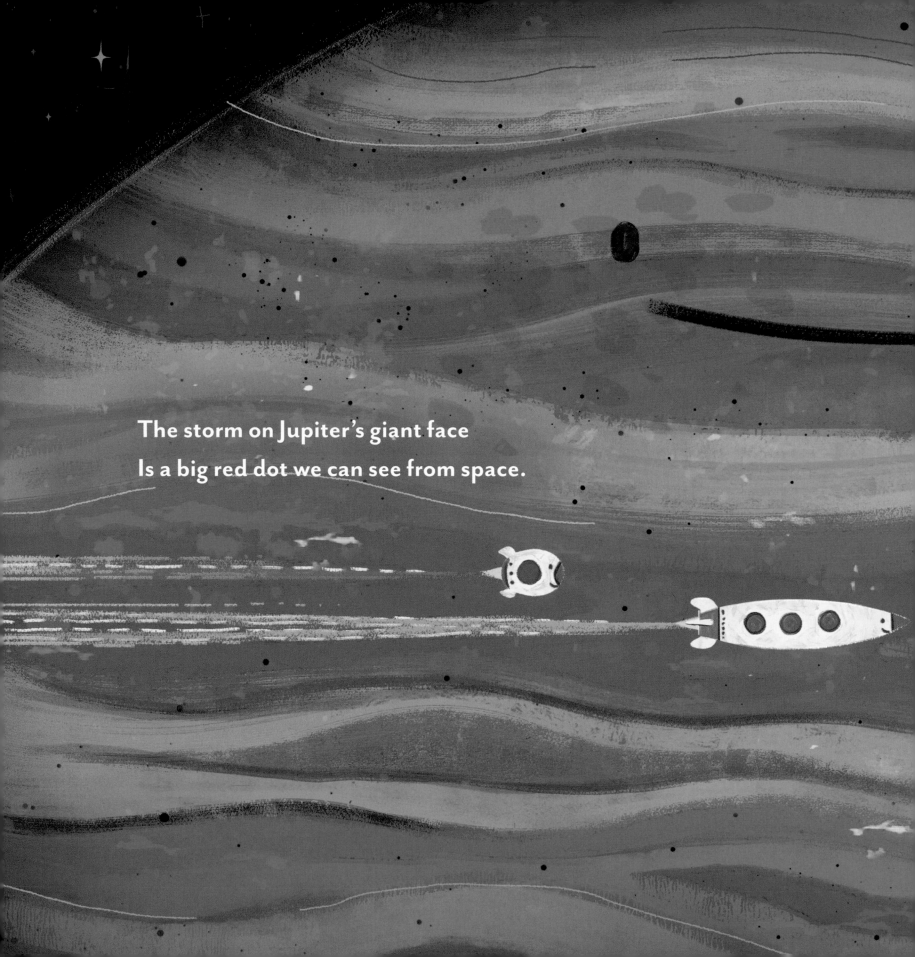

The storm on Jupiter's giant face
Is a big red dot we can see from space.

We wave to Saturn as we zoom
Past its rings and its many moons.

Uranus is tilted on one side.
It rolls round the sun on its orbit ride.

We see that Neptune looks so blue,

So we cheer it up with a joke or two.

Triton is Neptune's biggest moon.

We brush your windscreen sparkling bright.
We rub our nose cones and say, "Good night."

Tomorrow you'll play in the bright star beams.

Tonight, Little Rocket, have cosmic dreams.

Our **solar system** is our space neighborhood of eight planets and our sun.

It sits in the vast **Milky Way**, which is a spiral galaxy with over 100 billion stars in it.

Mercury is the closest to our sun and the smallest planet of our solar system. Some scientists think it's actually getting smaller. Its core is made of liquid, and as that cools, it becomes solid and shrinks.

Venus is the only planet in our solar system that spins clockwise and upside down. Some scientists believe that it was knocked over by another planet or large object far back in its history, and some believe that it flipped because of the effects of the sun's gravity and the planet's atmospheric tides. But whatever caused it to flip upside down, Venus is unique.

Earth's surface is about 70 percent water. Because of its oceans, astronauts say Earth looks like a big blue marble from space.

Mars has the largest mountain in the solar system. Olympus Mons has a diameter approximately the size of Arizona and may still be an active volcano.

Jupiter's red storm has been going on for at least 340 years. Jupiter's "Great Red Spot" is bigger than Earth!

Saturn has eighty-two moons (more than any other planet in our solar system), and its rings are made of pieces of rock and ice ranging from as small as a grain of sand to over half a mile across.

Uranus is tilted on its side. Astronomers think that it was knocked over long, long ago. Uranus was actually the first planet that was discovered using a telescope.

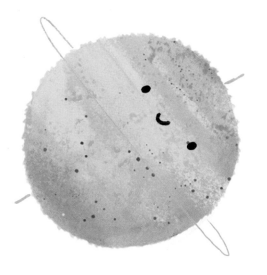

Neptune has stronger winds than any other planet in our solar system. The planet looks blue because of the methane in its atmosphere, which absorbs red. We have methane on Earth as well, in many forms—including cow toots! But we know there are absolutely no cows on Neptune. ☺

The **sun** is the biggest thing in our solar system, and it's so massive that about 1 million Earths could fit inside it.

The Earth's **moon** always shows Earth the same face as it rotates.

Even though sound doesn't travel through a vacuum, we all love **lunar lullabies!** ☺

To my own future space scientist, Charlotte. Thank you for sharing your ideas and your inspiration. You are my sunshine. —MO

To Zanna, for your wisdom, and Andrew, for your love, support, and endless supply of funny cat videos. —AC

A Feiwel and Friends Book
An imprint of Macmillan Publishing Group, LLC
120 Broadway, New York, NY 10271 · mackids.com

Our books may be purchased in bulk for promotional, educational, or business use.
Please contact your local bookseller or the Macmillan Corporate and Premium Sales Department
at (800) 221-7945 ext. 5442 or by email at MacmillanSpecialMarkets@macmillan.com.

Library of Congress Control Number: 2022910014

First edition, 2023
Book design by Mike Burroughs
The art for this book was created digitally using Photoshop and Procreate.
Feiwel and Friends logo designed by Filomena Tuosto
Printed in China by RR Donnelley Asia Printing Solutions Ltd.,
Dongguan City, Guangdong Province

ISBN 978-1-250-82806-4 (hardcover)
1 3 5 7 9 10 8 6 4 2